Favorite Pets
How to Choose and Care for Them

(Original title: Understanding Animals as Pets)

By Rita Vandivert

Photos by William Vandivert

SCHOLASTIC BOOK SERVICES
New York • Toronto • London • Auckland • Sydney • Tokyo

FOR BARNABY, PENELOPE
& SAMANTHA

No part of this publication may be reproduced in whole or in part, or stored in a retrieval system, or transmitted in any form or by any means, electronic, mechanical, photocopying, recording, or otherwise, without written permission of the publisher. For information regarding permission, write to Scholastic Book Services, 50 West 44th Street, New York, NY 10036.

ISBN: 0-590-08785-1

Text copyright © 1975 by Rita Vandivert. Photographs copyright © 1975 by William Vandivert. This abridged edition is published by Scholastic Book Services, a division of Scholastic Magazines, Inc., by arrangement with Frederick Warne & Co. The complete book UNDERSTANDING ANIMALS AS PETS is available at your bookstore or directly from FREDERICK WARNE & CO.

13 12 11 10 9 8 7 6 5 4   9/7 0 1 2 3 4/8

Printed in the U. S. A.

CONTENTS

How to Choose Your Pet   5

Your Pet Dog   10

Your Pet Cat   27

A Horse of Your Own   44

Small, Furry Pets   59

A Pet Bird   73

Snakes As Pets   84

Toads, Frogs, Turtles, or
   Lizards as Pets   92

How to Choose Your Pet

Which animal is the right one for me?
To find the answer to that important question, ask yourself another: Why do I want a pet?
There are many good reasons for wanting to have animals around you. They provide you with new interests. They make wonderful friends. They will give you their trust and affection, and are a lot of fun — if you treat them right.
But animals are not just playthings. If you get a camera for your birthday, you can enjoy it and then put it away on a shelf when your enthusiasm wanes. If you get a bicycle and the weather turns bad, you can forget it for months at a time. But animals are living creatures. They need your care and affection all the time.

So, you must be willing to take the responsibility for them and choose the kind of animal you can live with.

If you are an outdoor person with lots of energy, you will want an animal that can keep you company on walks and rides.

If your interests are in natural history or zoology, you can learn a lot by studying the animals that live with you. Animals are classed in groups and families. But when you get to know them well you discover they are individuals, too. They have their own ways of getting along with other animals and with you.

SELECTING YOUR FIRST PET

More likely than not, your first choice will be a **dog**. Almost everyone at some time has wished for a dog, and it is easy to understand why.

There are many kinds of dogs — all with different traits. So before you make up your mind which kind you want, think about what the dog will want from *you*, and whether you are willing to give him those things.

If you are not too keen on walking in bad weather, choose a small dog, one that will be happy in the house most of the time. Of course, any dog will need some fresh air, some walks and games both indoors and out — just as you do — but he will not need strenuous daily exercise all year around if he is one of the smaller breeds.

Jason, a handsome black Labrador, weighs well over 100 pounds. Although a city dog, he is in excellent shape because his owner takes him out every morning at six o'clock for an hour's run — and he gets four more runs throughout the day.

If you live in the country or the suburbs and love being in the open air, the sporting breeds and large dogs may be right for you. They not only love exercise, they must have plenty to keep healthy. And taking a dog for a walk is much more fun than going alone.

Whatever kind of dog you choose you will want him to obey you. If you have a disobedient dog, you may end up with more trouble than fun.

A horse or pony is, of course, an ideal animal to have in the country. But it takes time and work to keep a horse in good condition, and it takes a lot of money too.

Even if you have saved up enough to buy yourself a pony, or are lucky enough to have one bought for you, there is still his feed, his tack gear, his stabling, and veterinary care to be paid for. So seek out advice from people who keep horses before you get one, yourself.

Wherever you live, **cats** make wonderful pets. They are very different in their ways from dogs. They may not follow you about; often they may not do what you tell them — but they are good company and great fun.

Cats are individuals: no two are alike — not even kittens from the same family. Some may be livelier, some more mischievous, and others more friendly, real

Three eight-week-old Burmese kittens out in the sun with a grown-up friend of their mother.

lap cats. Although most cats like to go outdoors in good weather, there is no need to take them out regularly.

There are also many **smaller animals** that you can easily take care of in town or in the country, outdoors or in — little creatures like hamsters and gerbils, mice, rats, and guinea pigs. Provided with the right cage and the right food they can flourish and give you a lot of pleasure.

If you like cheerful noises and bright colors, there is a large variety of beautiful little **birds**. Originally imported from foreign countries, they have been bred to be kept in cages. Among the most popular are the parakeets, the cockateels, the lovebirds, and the canaries, as well as many gaily decorated little finches.

It certainly seems true that whatever your interests and wherever you live, you can find the right kind of pet or animal for you. The right pet is one that will not give you problems you cannot solve because you are not equipped to handle them. But this is not so difficult. Most animals are adaptable. If you take the trouble to determine what your animals need to keep healthy and content, they will usually meet you more than halfway.

Your Pet Dog

Becoming a dog owner is a pretty important step to take and needs talking over with the rest of the family. It is an even more important step for the dog. From the day you take him home, he is not only going to rely on you for his food, shelter, and exercises, but he is also going to need you to keep him healthy and show him how to get along with you, your family, other animals, and other people. Quite a responsibility! And what's in it for you? Anyone who has a dog that trusts him or her, has found a friend hard to equal.

There are many ways to become a dog owner. You may get a dog for a birthday present, your neighbors' dog may have a litter and they may offer you one of the puppies, or you may just happen to see one looking at you from a pet store window and not be able to pass it by. One very good way to obtain a dog is from your local Humane Society. There you can choose from a large selection of grown dogs and puppies, all of them really in need of a good home.

However, if there is a special breed of dog you want, one complete with pedigree, you should write to the American Kennel Club, 51 Madison Avenue, New York, New York 10010, and ask them to give you the name of a kennel which raises that breed in your part of the country. Then go to the kennel and get all the advice and information they will give you.

There are now six groups of recognized breeds in the United States. They all come from the types originally bred to serve man either as hunter, guard, tracker, sheepherder, sled dog, or friend. They are:

The Sporting Group: This covers spaniels, setters, pointers, retrievers, all dogs for the hunt.

A setter is an ideal companion for country life.

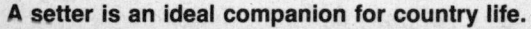

The Hounds: These are hunting dogs, too. They are trained to hunt by scent like bloodhounds, beagles, bassets, and dachshunds (otherwise known as badger dogs), and those who hunt by sight like greyhounds, whippets, salukis, and Afghans.

The Working Dogs: These are descendants of dogs originally trained to draw sleds, work with herds of cattle and flocks of sheep, or to act as guard dogs. They include the huskies, the collies and other sheep dogs, the St. Bernards, and the German shepherds.

The Terriers: Dogs trained originally to go ratting in farm country to protect the crops, but now mostly reared as pets — small but spunky types like the fox terrier, cairn, Scottish, Sealyham, and Skye.

The Toy Dogs: These are often miniature versions of larger breeds, pet dogs like the pug, the Pekingese, the Pomeranian, the Italian greyhound, the poodle, and the Chihuahua.

The Non-Sporting Dogs: The sixth group, dogs that do not fit into the other groups. This group contains some of the most popular dogs like the Dalmatian, poodle, bulldog, and Lhasa apso.

So look at the wide choice you have — from the tiny Mexican Chihuahua which can go into your pocket, to a Great Dane standing almost a yard high at the shoulder. Whatever your choice, you will understand the nature and behavior of your dog better if you keep in mind what his forebears were originally bred and trained to do, even though you are just looking for a good companion.

If you can pick your pup from a litter, there is no reason why you should not take home the one you fall in love with at first sight, but remember a few pointers. The puppy should not be separated from his mother before the age of six to eight weeks; a male dog will grow up larger and stronger; a female will usually be gentler and easier to train, but needs special care while she is "in heat" — the time she is capable of conceiving. If the dog's family is a pedigreed one, you will pretty well know what kind of dog your puppy will grow into, but highly bred dogs can be very nervous. If you choose from a mixed-breed family, you may not know so much about the parents of your dog, but he might turn out to be less temperamental than a blue blood.

BRINGING A NEW DOG HOME

When you first bring your dog home, have everything ready for him. A puppy needs a box or basket with a piece of rug or blanket. He likes his basket to be in a quiet spot, out of drafts, and always in the same place.

Like most dogs, Irving the dachshund likes to have his own basket — and his own toys.

Show him where his bowl of water and food will be kept, but let him have a good look around the house first. Do not expect him to eat right away.

Remember, all small puppies will chew anything handy. They will even swallow things that are bad for them, like stones, if they are not stopped in time. So keep him happy with a hard rubber toy, something that cannot injure him but will keep him busy.

If he is a grown-up dog and is going to live outdoors, have a sturdy kennel ready for him. Raise the floor a few inches from the ground, because dogs cannot stand dampness even though they don't mind the cold. Have the kennel face south and out of the wind. Place a piece of rug inside, and your dog will get along fine in most weather. If he is to be an outdoors dog, do not let him sleep indoors — unless he is ill, and then you should talk to the vet.

HOUSEBREAKING

If you bring home a puppy, you must start training him right away.

Take him outside every time he wakes up, after he eats or drinks, first thing in the morning, and last thing at night. If you are too late, scold him in a firm voice, but do not try punishing him — it simply will not work.

If he is quite small and it's not possible to whisk him outside, put down a newspaper in a corner, perhaps in the bathroom. Show him where it is right at the start; take him to it as often as you would take him outside. Change the newspaper when it gets used, but do not change the place. If he doesn't catch on right away, scold him each time, clean up the puddle, and show him the paper again. Whenever you get him there in time, pat him when he is through, and tell him he is a good dog. And when he finally trots over to the newspaper by himself, load him with pats and hugs and approval.

At about six months, you should be able to train him to go outdoors. Lead up to it gradually, take him out as often as you can, praise him when he does the right thing. But let him see that the newspaper is still in the corner in case he cannot wait until you are ready to take him out.

FEEDING

If you ask six different dog owners what they feed their pets, you will get six different answers. The truth is, there are many things that are good for dogs to eat, and several things they *like* to eat. One vet tells of a poodle fed large doses of blackstrap molasses for his nerves. The dog was in great shape when last heard of!

Here are some basic rules to follow:

1. When you bring a new dog home, find out what he *was* being fed and do not change that diet right away. Let the dog get accustomed to his strange surroundings before you start him on strange food — if you want to vary his meals.

2. Feed him at regular times, give him regular amounts and a corner of his own where a bowl of fresh water is kept, and let him eat his food in peace.

3. Give him food at room temperature, not food straight out of the refrigerator or still frozen.

4. Do not overfeed him — watch his weight.

"Food, please?" Schnauzers are hardy, active, intelligent, and affectionate.

There was a time when people thought dogs should be fed only raw meat and bones. Fortunately, since the price of meat is so high today, this is no longer considered an ideal diet. Most of the makers of prepared pet foods provide a balanced diet containing protein, minerals, and vitamins. What's more, they have consulted the dogs to see how they like the formulas. They keep permanent kennels of different dogs and cats and let them indicate preferences. Prepared foods come in three forms: canned meat, fish, or chicken; semi-moist patties or chunks; and dry food like biscuits and pellets. The patties are fine for young dogs and small breeds, but get expensive for larger animals. The dry food is economical and good as part of the daily diet for any dog.

It is still true that bones are good for a dog's teeth, but bones can splinter. A perfectly safe bone is a beef shin bone. Boil it in plenty of water, scrape any meat off and push out the marrow. Give meat and marrow to the dog, then boil the bone until it is white. One shin bone can keep your puppy chewing away until he is a full-grown dog.

WEANING PUPPIES

While a mother dog is nursing her puppies she should have extra food and some milk. As soon as the pups start to stagger around (at about three weeks) and can

Sasha, half Pyrenees, half collie, had her first litter at thirteen months. Her pups are just under three weeks old.

eat from a dish, try giving them milk, beaten egg and milk, or a little cereal with milk. Later try a little scraped beef, raw liver, or cottage cheese, then gradually get the pups on canned food. By the time they are six to eight weeks old, they should be weaned and getting four or five meals a day. At six months, three meals a day are enough, two meals by the time they are a year old. While they are growing fast they need plenty to eat. Once they are grown, do not overfeed them.

GROOMING

If you fell for the charms of a long-haired dog when you chose your puppy, you will have to work to keep him neat and clean. Short-haired dogs should be brushed several times a week, and some terrier types need plucking to remove dead hairs. Schnauzers and poodles do not shed their hair. This spares the sofas and chairs, but means they should go to the dog barber for a trim every few months.

Long-haired dogs must be combed carefully to keep the hair free from tangles, and then they should be brushed to make their coats shine. Even if you don't comb them every day, do it often enough to avoid matting. Mats are tricky to comb out without hurting the dog's feelings as well as his appearance.

Left, Kermit, a five-year-old cairn terrier, holds still for a brushing.
Right, Brushing done, he is ready to go for his 3- times-a-day walk.

Dogs should not be bathed often, but their bedding should be kept clean. If your dog gets himself really dirty and has to have a bath, it will take two people to do it properly. Use warm water and mild soap or dog shampoo. Plug his ears with cotton and be careful not to get the soapy water in his eyes. Rinse him in clean water and dry him with a thick towel. If he is a small fellow you can use a hair dryer if there is one in the family. Be sure he is quite dry before he gets in a draft or goes out, particularly in cold weather.

Your dog's nails should be cut every so often, including the dew claws — the nails up the foot that do not touch the ground. A dog barber will take care of this and if you watch the barber closely, you can get a dog's nail trimmer and do it yourself. But go very carefully. If he is a real outdoor dog and gets plenty of exercise, his nails will not need much cutting.

HEALTH

It is really not difficult to keep your dog healthy. He needs the same things you do to keep fit—a good, balanced diet, plenty of fresh air, exercise, and playtime, and a certain amount of grooming.

If you have a yard, field, or garden, or live near a park in the city, take him out twice a day, unless the weather is too bad. Throw sticks or a ball so that he gets tired before you do.

All large dogs need a lot of exercise. You can put them on a leash with a ring which slides along a stretched wire, but they are going to be happier, friendlier dogs if they have company as much of the time as possible. Dogs get lonely.

At first puppies just need to be played with for exercise. Fresh air is good for them too. But you cannot expect them to go walking far with you before they are four or five months old.

The most important thing about your new puppy's health is to be sure he has the necessary inoculations against distemper. Ask about shots he has already had when you get him, then check with the vet to see how often he needs the temporary "puppy" shots and later, the longer-lasting dose.

Keep your dog clean, bright-eyed, and alert and he will be fine. His eyes and ears may need attention occasionally. Wipe his eyes with a piece of damp cotton if they look gooey; wipe his ears out with cotton dipped in a little mineral oil to keep them clean. If he shakes his head often or his ears seem to bother him, check with a vet. In fact, checking with your vet is a very good idea whenever you think there may be something not quite right with your dog. It may be something you can take care of yourself, once the vet provides you with salve or medicine, but if the trouble does not clear up get him to the vet, the sooner the better.

TRAINING

All dogs need some training if they are not going to make your life and theirs a misery. So remember these six things:

1. Your dog has enough intelligence to learn, if he has a good teacher. Almost all dogs *want* to learn, and they *want* to please you. If you praise them for doing things your way, they will go along with you. But you must be fair, you must be firm, you must make yourself clear.

2. Though your puppy at first may do things he shouldn't, like running away, jumping on furniture or on people, knocking things over, chewing things up, he is not being deliberately naughty. He needs to be shown exactly what he may do and what he must not

These dogs, sitting in line, are so well trained they will not move until given the command.

do, but rough treatment toward a puppy may spoil his nature for the rest of his life.

3. Dogs do not speak English, but you can teach them the meaning of some words. To begin with, give your dog a name, and he should soon learn to respond to it. After his name the most important words are COME—SIT—DOWN—STAY—HEEL, and to release him from these, OKAY. Keep to single words, not chatty sentences, or else you will confuse him. He will also go by the sound of your voice, so smile and say GOOD DOG pleasantly when he obeys. Use a sterner tone when he disobeys, but do not shout.

4. Dogs can only associate praise or punishment with whatever they have *just* been doing. If he runs away and you hit him when he comes back, he connects the punishment with the coming back and not with the running away.

5. Do not let him get away with undesirable behavior when he is little and cute—like sitting on you when he is muddy or jumping up on your clean shirt—that you won't put up with when he is full grown. Start right.

6. Dogs cannot concentrate for too long, so keep the lessons short and stop before the dog gets tired or loses interest. Little and often is best. Dogs are easily distracted by things going on around them. Things you might not notice are often enough to take their minds off the job.

TIME TO BEGIN

Apart from housebreaking your dog, which you want to do as soon as possible, let him get to know and trust you before you attempt to teach him other things.

You can put a collar on your puppy as soon as you like. Just give him time to get used to it before you introduce him to his leash, and be sure to change the collar for a bigger one as he grows.

When you think he is ready—and this depends on the dog—you can begin to train him to heel. A check collar is a great help at this stage, because it tightens if he pulls or drags, but is comfortable if he stays at your side. Keep him on a short leash at your left side. If he goes ahead of you, scold him, and pull him back firmly. If he drags, pull him toward you. When he stays at your

This young dog was a stray of mixed parentage, but caught on quickly to the idea of walking to heel.

side, pat him and say GOOD DOG! Keep this up for short bouts several times a day, and soon he should get the idea.

How much more you can teach him depends upon both you and your dog. If you are patient and kind and your instructions are clear, the dog will come to understand you. Always remember the object of the training—to prevent the dog from being a nuisance to you, your family, and your friends—not to show how smart you are.

You want to arrive at an understanding with your dog so that he will come when you call his name, walk at your side, sit when you tell him to, stay put when you say STAY, until you release him with the word OKAY or COME.

There are groups all over the country which give obedience classes to dog owners, often free. And there are classes where you pay each time you go. In class together both dog owners and dogs can learn a lot from each other.

BREEDING VERSUS NEUTERING

If you have a registered female dog and want her to have a family, get in touch with the American Kennel Club, or the dog's original owner, or the kennel she came from. They will put you in touch with dogs to father the pups and give you other advice. However, the mating, the care of the pregnant mother, the birth of the pups, and their early care are all quite complicated. And it is most important that you know beforehand that you will have good homes for every one of the puppies.

There are millions of dogs today, including pedigrees, who have no home, and will probably end up in animal shelters and eventually be killed. This happens every day in every city throughout the country.

Neutering dogs is the sensible way to prevent unwanted animals from being born. Your vet will do this, or there are clinics which perform these simple operations to help slow up the dog population, so that those already born will stand a better chance of finding a good home.

This well-trained standard poodle walks without a leash beside a three-year-old.

Your Pet Cat

Elegant is the word for cats. Consider some other members of the family, the African lion, the Bengal tiger and, perhaps the most beautiful of all cats, the snow leopard, who lives in the world's highest mountains. Unfortunately, some of these magnificent beasts are disappearing from their natural haunts. Our only hope of not losing them forever is through the work pursued by several zoos, who breed the animals in captivity.

There is no likelihood that our domestic cats will disappear; their problem is the opposite one. There are far too many cats, and always more on the way. So there will be no difficulty obtaining a cat or kitten if you want one. Throughout the United States, Humane Societies, the A.S.P.C.A., and like organizations are taking temporary care of thousands of cats, hoping they will be offered permanent homes.

Of course if your kitten comes from a mother cat you already know, you will have some idea how healthy or easily trained your kitten will be. But it will not necessarily be like its parents, any more than children are. For cats are highly individual creatures.

You can also buy a cat or kitten from a pet shop. There you will have a choice of many kinds and colors: white, red, blue, cream or smoky, calico or tortoise shell, long-haired or short-haired, cats with kinky tails, and cats with no tail at all.

The fancy members of the family such as Siamese, Persian, Burmese, Abyssinian, or Russian Blue come with long pedigrees and cost a lot of money. The cat does not care about its pedigree, but if you plan to breed a purebred cat you must keep the papers.

Wherever you get your kitten, beware of runny noses or a sickly look. You will be much happier with your pet if it is healthy and playful. A sick kitten needs much extra care, and you will be brokenhearted if it doesn't make it.

CAT VERSUS KITTEN

Most people find all kittens irresistible, but they sometimes forget that, with luck, every kitten is going to become a cat. So, if you do not like cats, do not get a kitten.

Gina calls her silvery tabby kitten Matisse. She holds him carefully and he plays gently, too.

Kittens less than six weeks old are too young to be taken from their mothers. After that, they need special care to begin with, but you have the marvelous experience of watching them grow and develop and learn.

If you start with a grown cat, he might be less bother than a young kitten is. He might, if you are lucky, be a well-trained cat, and he will probably not rush around your home as wildly as a youngster.

MALE VERSUS FEMALE

At the kitten stage, male and female cats do not seem to differ much. But they do as they grow up. As a rule a female will be a gentler animal, except perhaps when she has kittens. Males are usually bigger and tougher and more likely to roam. In either case, if you are not going to breed your cat, have it neutered. There are more details about this on page 40.

WHAT CATS LIKE

Cats like warmth, comfort, affection, attention, and a place they can call their own. When they come to a new home, they like you to talk quietly to them, stroke them from stem to stern and then leave them alone for a while to explore their new surroundings.

Before you let them wander, take care to close windows at the bottom, closet doors, and outside doors, too. Put a little bowl of milk or water and some food where they can see it — the kitchen is usually a good place — but do not worry if they are too busy looking around to stop for food or drink.

Show your kittens the litter pan you have ready for them and a box or basket where they can curl up comfortably. Line the box with an old piece of blanket or towel, something easily washable, and put the box in a warm corner away from drafts.

Kittens are often scared when they first leave the close quarters of a pet shop cage or the coziness of a basket with their mother and brothers and sisters. They may go looking for somewhere they feel secure in, and it may not be an easy place to spot. If they disappear, try looking under beds and other low furniture, in cupboards or closets or on shelves, and if they are still missing, try behind the refrigerator or the stove. When you find them, put them back in their beds, tell them how nice they are and how silly it was to be scared.

We brought home a little Siamese kitten from a pet

Our Siamese cat Samantha loves to climb.

store, and at first she spent her time under chairs or beds or cushions. When we picked her up, she would take one glance down and see how far away the floor was, then let out a mighty yell — well, a large yell for a small kitten. Since those days she has the entire apartment mapped out to her liking.

Cats also like high places; sitting on mantelpieces or bookshelves makes them feel very good because they can look you in the eye instead of watching your feet all the time.

Cats like to play games, even when they are grown up. This is one reason why it is a good idea to start with two cats or kittens instead of one. A pair of kittens growing up together have an endless amount of fun and are wonderful to watch. Even a dignified older cat will, given time, be won over by the antics of a new kitten and join the game.

If you have only one cat, you are expected to be the playmate. But remember it is the cat who makes the rules — and changes them. Fortunately, very simple things and inexpensive toys are all cats need for play. Empty reels of thread, small balls — ones with a bell inside are very good — crunched-up pieces of paper stiff enough to rustle, a catnip mouse, all will amuse your cat when he is ready to play. A good toy can be made from a small brown paper bag folded over several times until it is about 1 x 3 inches, then strongly tied around the middle with a stout piece of string. Leave a long end to the string and walk around the room dragging the paper behind you. When the cat decides to join in, get up speed, and the cat will do the rest. Some cats are so fond of this game that they will bring the toy to

Cats will make a great game of hiding and playing in grocery bags.

you in their mouths and lay it at your feet (broad hint). We have seen only Siamese cats do this retrieving act, but there may well be others that do it too.

While kittens are ready to make toys out of anything they come across, you should keep some things away from them, like rubber bands, pens, pencils, or thin string — anything small enough for them to swallow.

There are other hazards to look out for. Cats are so curious they have to know what is going on, and accidents can happen. They love to sit and look out a window, which is fine as long as the window is shut, but if it is left open at the bottom, they may venture out onto the sill and fall. Any open door invites them to look around, whether it belongs to a closet, a cellar, an oven, or a refrigerator. Anything with a lid off or open, whether a suitcase or a can of paint, is too tempting to pass by. And in a house where the cat can get outdoors, he is likely to wander right out into the street. Many cats are killed this way.

HOUSEBREAKING

It is natural for a cat to keep himself spick and span, and be quickly housebroken. For an inside cat, the simplest setup is a shallow pan, plastic or enamel, containing an inch or two of shredded newspaper or cat litter. Always show a new cat where the pan is kept. The bathroom is a good place, or some quiet corner. Cats like privacy.

They also like something in the pan they can scratch to cover up their traces. (This is instinctive; their wild ancestors did not want their enemies to find them.) Try to keep the pan in one place, but if you have to move it, be sure to show them where it is. Keep it clean — changing it about once a day. If a newly arrived cat or kitten has an accident, scolding or punishing it will simply scare and confuse it. Thoroughly clean the spot they used, show them the pan again, and put them right by it after they have eaten or had a drink. Most cats catch on right away.

If your cat can use the outdoors, you may still have to start off with an indoor pan, particularly if you have a small kitten and the weather is bad. But over a period of time, you can get him accustomed to going outside. Start by putting the cat out after each meal and last thing at night, and before long he will tell you when to open the door for him. Some cats seem to take particular delight in having you open the door to let them out, then calling you right back again to let them in. If you tire of this before they do, you can construct a cat door — have a small hinged section made at the base of a back door, through which the cat can come and go by himself. He may not find it fun at first, but eventually he will use it. If he is free to come and go, however, remember he can climb and jump and sneak through very small places, so be careful you do not lose him.

FEEDING

Healthy cats take quite a lot of interest in their food. They often have definite ideas about when and what they should eat. It is up to you to see that they grow up with good eating habits, so start out right.

Young kittens should have plenty of milk with a little warm water added. Ice-cold food or drink is not good for them, nor for grown-up cats. You can feed kittens three times a day, or more. Kittens, unlike puppies, will not overeat. When they reach six months, three meals a day is enough, two meals a day for a mature cat. Never let your cats get fat.

Canned foods are good as a rule, but read the small print on the label. Check to see that the cans contain vitamins and minerals, and have a *low ash content*. This last is very important for males. You can offer your cat canned fish, meat, chicken, or various mixtures, and you will probably find he has his own preferences. Go along with him to a degree, but it is important to keep his diet varied. Especially avoid a steady tuna diet.

Cats should never be fed at family meals, but if they flock to the kitchen when the food is being put away, a few leftovers will please them. They like bits of chicken, fish, meat, liver, kidney (raw or cooked), but do not risk giving them bones of any kind.

Dry cat food in various flavors is good occasionally,

and usually popular — most cats come running when they hear the crisp nuggets fall into their dish. After eating dry food they will want a drink of water, just as we like something liquid with cookies or other dry food. In fact, always have a bowl of fresh water handy for cats, just as you would for a dog.

Mature cats do not need milk. Some veterinarians do not recommend it. But cats will sometimes want to drink milk if they are off their feed or getting over an illness and aren't feeling robust.

If your cat does not get outdoors into a yard or garden, add a shredded lettuce leaf to its canned food. If you do not do this, the cat will probably eat your house plants, since every so often it feels the need for something green.

GROOMING

A well-brushed cat, long-haired or short-haired, looks elegant and has far fewer hairs to shed all over your

clothes and furniture. And if you start brushing a kitten from the first day you get it, it will love having its coat brushed. Regular brushing helps prevent hairballs.

Your cat keeps himself clean, so he never needs a bath unless he accidentally gets into some mess he cannot get off by himself. When this happens, use warm water, mild soap, and a large cloth, but do not try it single-handed. He will not like the treatment and might scratch.

If he is not an outdoors cat, he needs his claws clipped from time to time. This again takes two of you, and you need a pair of cat-nail clippers. One of you holds him firmly on a table, two hands on his back to press him down; the other one, ready with the clippers, takes up one paw at a time and presses gently to make the claws come out. You must clip only the extreme tip of the claw, and be very careful not to cut the tiny red vein which you can see extending into the claw. Front paws are the most important, but clip the back ones too if the cat holds still. But rather than get the cat too angry, leave the back claws for another time.

Some people avoid clipping by having the claws completely removed. If asked, the cats would prefer not to have this happen — it leaves them quite defenseless. Cats that will be going outdoors should never have their claws removed.

◀ **Big Kate is a purebred Persian, well-groomed, and well brushed. Persians are best kept as indoor pets; their long, silky fur mats easily with dirt and stickers.**

You have to face the fact that as soon as you clip his claws the cat will look around for something to resharpen them on. If you want to spare your furniture, you must provide the cat with something he *may* scratch. You can get a scratching post from the pet store provided it is sturdy. You can also make your own. Bring in a small chunk of a fallen tree with the bark still on it, or cover a small log with a piece of carpet. We make a device of our own that works even better. We take a piece of wood about a foot wide and two or three feet long. We pad it with felt and cover it tightly with a piece of coarsely woven cloth which we staple down. We secure this firmly on a wall, one where the cat often goes (the kitchen), and you can see her making very good use of her scratching board in the photograph. You must attach it high enough to allow the cat to stretch full length without reaching the top.

Samantha is provided with a steady scratching pad which helps save the furniture.

DRESSING

When they were worshipped as gods nearly five thousand years ago, ancient Egyptian cats wore resplendent collars, necklaces, and earrings. Although cats are beautiful without such adornment, there are times when it is a good idea to provide your cat with a collar. If he is inclined to wander, you can buy metal collar attachments on which his name and address can be engraved. You can also get a collar with a bell attached. At first the cat will not like the bell, but he will get used to it. Birds have a better chance to get away if he is a bird chaser.

You really should not punish him if he does catch birds, since it is his nature. After all, cats' first usefulness to man was to save the stores of grain from rats and mice, and we still approve of cats catching them. So it is hard for cats to understand why mice are fair game and birds are not.

Cats do not need coats. Those that spend time outdoors during cold weather grow their own thick woolly coats.

HEALTH

If you start off with a healthy cat it is not difficult to keep him in good shape.

A very infectious disease called feline enteritis used to cause the death of thousands of cats. Nowadays inoculations at the right time bring most cats through this and other dangers. Find out exactly what shots, if any, your kitten has been given before you had him. Then check with your vet who will tell you when to bring the kitten in for any further shots.

Brushing your cat will lessen the risk of his swallowing too much hair, which collects into balls inside him and causes constipation. Give him a weekly small spoonful of olive oil or salad oil when necessary. If he refuses the oil and spills it over you and himself, try smearing a dab of petroleum jelly on his nose and front paws, which he will lick off. This, or an ointment you can buy at the pet store, helps him lubricate himself.

Eyes and ears should be watched. Eyes can be wiped gently with a piece of dampened cotton, but do not touch his ears. If he shakes his head and scratches his outer ears a lot, this may mean he has ear mites, which are very irritating. For this, and for any other trouble you do not understand, take him to the vet.

NEUTERING

Neutering male cats and spaying female cats has everything to recommend it. Remember the millions of surplus cats in the world and think very carefully before bringing in more. The operation is a simple one, and should be done within the first year of a cat's life. Males can go home from the vet's the same day, while females must stay over at least one night. The cats recover quickly and there is little change in their temperaments — except for the better. The males will no longer spray your furniture or walls, and they will not fight so much. The females will not howl or try to get away as they do normally when they come into heat.

BREEDING AND CARING FOR A MOTHER CAT AND KITTENS

Of course if you have a pedigreed cat you may want to breed her, or you may like the idea of letting your cat, however humble her origins, have one batch of kittens before you have her spayed. If you do that, be sure in advance that all the kittens will have good homes.

As the time approaches for the kittens to appear — about nine weeks after mating — feed her well and handle her gently. Put a box or basket lined with something soft in a quiet spot and show it to her. If you are

This alley cat mother fostered 2 orphaned bobcat kittens in addition to nursing her own kitten, the black one in the middle. He got along fine with his wild relations.

lucky, she will use it, but watch where she goes in case she has other ideas.

Just before giving birth the cat may show signs of nervousness, refuse her food, and stay in her bed. If you could read her mind at this stage, you would undoubtedly find she was telling you to leave her alone.

Giving birth usually takes the mother about two hours from the first to the last kitten, but it can take a lot longer than that, depending on the cat, and sometimes as many as four kittens can arrive in half an hour.

As each kitten emerges head first, it is inside a thin transparent cover called the amniotic sac. The mother cat removes this with her teeth and tongue, then bites off the umbilical cord. This is how she separates the kitten from the placenta, the material by which the unborn kitten has been nourished. Next she licks the kitten vigorously all over, which helps it to start breathing. Usually the mother cat tidies up after each kitten by eating the sac and the placenta and lapping up the amniotic fluid. If she doesn't, you can clean the bed up for her later, but do not handle the newborn kittens as they arrive. Give the mother the opportunity to take care of everything herself. She is very good at it. The best thing you can do for her is to have fresh water and some slightly warmed milk nearby.

The kittens will start nursing on the mother right away and will continue for about four weeks. Then you and she together can wean the kittens. Before that time, particularly during the first two weeks when their eyes are closed, do not disturb kittens or mother any more than necessary.

Once the kittens are weaned, give them as much warm milk as they will drink, either fresh or diluted evaporated milk. Gradually add small quantities of cat food to their diet four times a day. Increase the amount and reduce the number of meals to three a day once they are three months old.

If your cat is a registered female and you want to breed pedigreed kittens, get advice from the pet shop or breeder where you got her. And if you just want to talk cats and compare notes with other cat lovers, there are more than three hundred cat clubs throughout the United States, from the Crown Jewel Cat Club in Atlanta, Georgia, to the Totem Cat Club in Tacoma, Washington.

Albert came from a Bide-a-Wee shelter as a kitten. Now, at six, he is a handsome, lovable cat — "every inch a gentleman."

A Horse of Your Own

The pleasures of horseback riding are easy to see; the many responsibilities (as well as expenses) that go with owning a horse are not so obvious. You should allow yourself a period of preparation before you decide definitely to have a horse of your own. If you start off well prepared you can have endless good times. You will take pride in sitting up straight in the saddle and looking down on the rest of the world, or training yourself and your mount for the excitement of show jumping.

You can do all this once you understand your horse well, and have expert control of him so that he has confidence in you and your abilities and does your bidding. It takes quite a while to become an accomplished rider, and starting young is a great help.

One of the best ways to get into the horse scene is to find out all you can about the local 4-H Club horse activities in your state. The programs vary from state to state but they may include instruction on horsemanship and horse management, and visits to nearby farms and stables. Some 4-H clubs put on shows, judging contests, and demonstrations.

Another way to get started is to make friends with the lucky people who already have horses. Watch them and their horses, and if you see they ride well and take proper care of their animals, you know you are onto a good thing.

Members of a 4-H Club horse group are shown how to saddle a horse. Cindy Lou shows them how to get the length of the stirrup leather right —by measuring her arm's length.

Next, offer to help groom the horses. Grooming is great fun to begin with, but somebody who has had a mount of his own for some time is often happy to have a little help with the dirty part of the job. This kind action on your part could lead to the offer of a ride!

Meantime you should, if possible, take riding lessons. You can take them from a grownup who is fond of horses and has had a lot of experience with them. Or you can sign up for lessons at a riding stable to learn the basic steps. Practice riding with others, and pick up all the horse lore you can from the instructor and the other pupils.

It is great fun getting to know the inner mysteries of horse care. "Horsey" people set great store in having everything called by its right name. This is the sort of thing you should know — for example, *tack* means all the gear your horse wears: saddle, bridle, halter, etc. And the place where they are kept is the *tack room*.

Julia is cleaning Penny's saddle with saddle soap. She still has stirrup leather to wash and polish, and the stirrups and bit have to be cleaned and shined.

You only talk about *harnessing* a horse if it is one that pulls a cart of some kind, not one that is for riding. Remember, too, that the left side of a horse must be called the *near* side, and the right side is the *off* side.

There are many other pieces of equipment which come under the heading of tack, with lovely romantic names like martingale, surcingle, hackamore, snaffle, and half-moon pelham bit. It may be fun getting to know all the right names, but it is serious work to keep them all clean and in tip-top condition. They should be washed with saddle soap, the metal parts brightly polished, and everything kept in a dry clean place when not in use.

And when you get to the stage where you are allowed the privilege of cleaning the stable, whatever you may think of the job, refer to it as *mucking out*.

GROOMING

Grooming means any kind of brushing, cleaning, or generally tidying up your horse, and you need special equipment to do it. First of all you should have a dandy brush to give the horse a good stiff brushing (the way of the hair). Then you need a body brush, which you use with a circular motion in one hand, holding a curry-comb in your other hand. The comb is to clean the brush, not the horse. Other tools are a hoof pick, sponges, mane and tail comb (use it gently, don't tug),

Getting Penny ready for a ride. She gets her coat thoroughly brushed.

and a duster or rubber for giving the coat a final polish.

Watch the whole procedure done by someone who really knows the ropes, and if he hisses while he works — which is to soothe the horse and at the same time keep the dust out of his own mouth — you will know you are watching an expert.

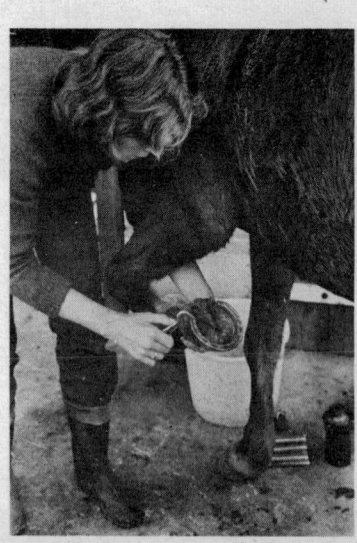

Using the hoof pick after a ride, in case there are any small stones lodged between hoof and shoe.

RIDING STYLE

Before getting tack of your own you will have to choose your riding style. Perhaps your choice will depend upon how your friends ride, and where you take riding lessons. The choice is between Western and English. Once you make up your mind, you will know what tack both you and your horse will need.

Western style means using a cowboy saddle. A good one should have a leather-covered horn, never a metal spike, which is dangerous, and it should have hooded stirrups. This type of saddle cannot be used for jumping. You will guide your horse by *neck reining*, which means using the rein against the side of his neck. When the left rein touches the horse's neck he turns to the right, and vice versa. You will get yourself up in blue jeans, shirt, scarf or tie, and a cowboy hat to protect your head.

In the *English* style there are two kinds of saddle. With a flat saddle you sit well back, you *post* when the horse trots, and you use a bridle with double reins. You guide your horse by pulling on the leading rein (right one) to turn him to the right, and on the left rein to go left.

The alternate saddle for English style is the hunt seat, which is designed for jumping, whereas the flat saddle is for the show ring, or just for trail riding.

In English style your outfit is usually more formal —

Practice jumping — Welsh pony and rider — English style.

jodhpurs or breeches, and a jacket, and also a hard hat which is essential for jumping.

Whatever else you fancy in the way of riding habit, you should wear boots with any costume — they protect you both on your horse and in the stable.

Of course there is a lot more to learn about riding properly. And a lot more about the tack, too. As a beginner, be sure to have an experienced rider check you out carefully each time you saddle and bridle your horse before you take off.

WHICH HORSE IS BEST FOR YOU?

Once you have been spending time around horses long enough to know something about them, perhaps you feel ready to have a horse of your own. At this point some serious figuring with your parents is called for.

You will have realized that, quite apart from the original cost of the horse — which can be considerable — there will be many expensive things to buy in order to provide him with tack and shelter. Then, after that, there will be a steady outlay of money for food and regular veterinary care.

Whenever possible, it is best to buy a horse or pony from friends, or at least through a source well recommended by an experienced friend. Auctions and horse dealers should be avoided, except in the company of an experienced guide.

Let it be known that you are looking for a horse or pony. Talk to people at local riding clubs or stables. Here again the 4-H Club group can be of help. Also, there are several good horse and pony magazines published in different states which will have information about sales and other affairs.

Julia with her chestnut mare, Penny, and a new Welsh pony called Pepe. Pepe, only a year and a half old, is too young to be ridden but keeps Penny from getting lonely.

At a horse and pony fair — a good place to find out how horses are bought and sold.

POINTS

When you are buying, it is essential to have someone with you who is no greenhorn, who knows what points to look for, what to avoid, and what questions to ask.

Even if you fall for a particular pony, take your time before leading him home. Watch how he behaves when somebody goes into his stall, when he is being groomed, when he is led to pasture, or caught for bringing back in. Ask to be allowed to try these tests for yourself and then, if you are satisfied that the pony is quite manageable, as a final step ask the owner politely why he is selling the pony and what faults he has. He may or may not tell you. In any case, have the veterinarian check the horse before you agree to buy him.

SIZE

This is important, because you want a mount the right size for your height. You will want to be comfortable astride and feel you look good, but you don't want to feel so far from the ground that you are afraid of falling. And, you should be able to saddle, bridle, and groom the horse yourself.

Here again, you must get your terms right. Most young riders start on a pony, which is a mount that is not more than fourteen hands high. A *hand* is four inches; the animal is measured from the *withers* (the area between the neck and shoulders) down to the ground. Over 14.2 hands your mount is a horse. However, whatever size an Arab is, the animal will be called a horse, never a pony; and whatever size a polo mount is. it is a pony and never a horse. A Shetland pony, the smallest breed, is the only one measured in inches, not in hands.

AGE

Ponies can live for twenty-five years or more, so you have a wide choice of age. Young ones, two or three years old, may seem a bargain because they are cheaper than older ones. If you pick out a youngster, you must be prepared to train it and cope with its frisky behavior, since there is no way of telling whether he is a naturally calm or an excitable creature until schooling begins. A pony of seven years or more is considered in its prime and, provided it is sound in wind and limb, will probably give you a quieter ride and a better opportunity to gain confidence.

WHAT IS BEST FOR YOUR HORSE?

If you do not have suitable space to house your horse or pony comfortably, you may have to board him at a stable or riding academy nearby. This is costly and not as satisfying as taking care of him yourself to insure he is properly looked after.

Before you bring your horse home you must have his quarters ready for him.

Hardy ponies grow thick winter coats and can live outdoors most of the time, but they do need shelter from bitter cold winds and drifting snow as well as protection from flies and heat. The best arrangement is a stable with an adjoining paddock where he can graze and be exercised. You can also adapt a shed or garage if it will be dry and free from drafts, or you can buy a horse's stall ready-made.

If you have the building, but no paddock, you should rent a grazing area from a farmer, and if there are other horses there to keep him company, so much the better. But each horse must have at least an acre of ground to feed in.

Whatever arrangement you make for indoors or out,

where you keep your pony should not be far from home. You want to get to him easily, spend plenty of time with him, talk to him frequently, and you want him to be accessible in cold or wet weather.

His food supplies, bedding, blankets, and tack are going to take up a lot of room, too. You really need a separate area to keep the tack in, and if you have ample room for the bedding straw and the hay, you can buy these in larger quantities and save money.

Penny has her own stall — with a "window" so that she can see what's going on.

FOOD AND WATER

A horse spends much time feeding himself, sometimes twenty hours out of the twenty-four, so make sure he has good grass if he is outdoors and a regular supply of other food when he is stabled. Quantities vary according to the size of the animal, the amount of exercise he gets, and how much of his time is spent in or out. As a rule the haynet in the stable should be filled morning and night — loose hay is wasteful — and most horses need crushed oats or grain mixtures as well. If he is stabled most of the time during the winter months, he should get a feed of warm bran mash once a week.

All horses drink a lot of water, so a brook running through your pasture is a great asset. Otherwise you must always keep a good supply of fresh clean water available both during the day and through the night. Rainwater is good, but no water should be icy cold in winter. If you use a bucket, make sure it is a heavy wooden one that the horse will not knock over, and rinse it out each time you refill it. He should drink before he eats, not immediately after, nor when he is hot and sweaty after exercise.

On top of all the tack you have collected, do not forget the equipment to keep the stable clean. You need such things as a fork, a spade, a good stiff broom, and a wheelbarrow to carry out the manure, because a healthy horse is one that is groomed regularly and lives in clean surroundings.

HORSE SENSE

With proper equipment and regular care your pony should stay not only happy but healthy, too. However, if he goes off his feed, runs lame, or shows any other signs of distress, you should call in the vet. Do not try to doctor him yourself.

What you can do best of all for your horse is to understand him and be truly a friend. Horses are timid by nature, and not always clever at reasoning things out for themselves. Sudden noises scare them, so always approach slowly and talk softly. They do not understand what you say, let's face it, but they are sensitive to the tone of your voice. If something frightens them out in the open, they want to steer clear of it, so lead a horse quietly by whatever it is that is bothering him and let him see it is harmless.

Indoors, horses may kick or bite if they are cornered and scared, particularly if previously they have been badly treated and have become ill-tempered. If this is the case you have a problem on your hands, yet waving a whip and shouting is not going to achieve positive results. Time and patience may give the pony sufficient confidence in you to lose his fears and, eventually, behave better.

If you keep calm, your pony will too, and if you are scared, he will sense this. It is understandable that you may feel a little afraid of a new pony. After all he has strong teeth, hard hooves, and is bigger than you are.

So the thing to do is move quietly, show your fondness for him, talk pleasantly to him, and he will respond. Remember that until he gets to know you he is scared of you, too. But kindness will work wonders and you will both gain confidence in each other.

And don't worry too much about falling off. Most long-time riders cannot claim they have never fallen off a horse, so always wear a hard hat. If you think you are going to fall, free your feet of the stirrups, but try to hang on to the reins; go limp and try to roll off on the softest spot. Then pick yourself up and get right back on the horse.

Human companionship is very important to a horse, and the more friendliness he gets the more knowing he will become. Spend plenty of time with him, talk to him when you groom and saddle him, and when you go off for a fine ride together, sing as you both go along.

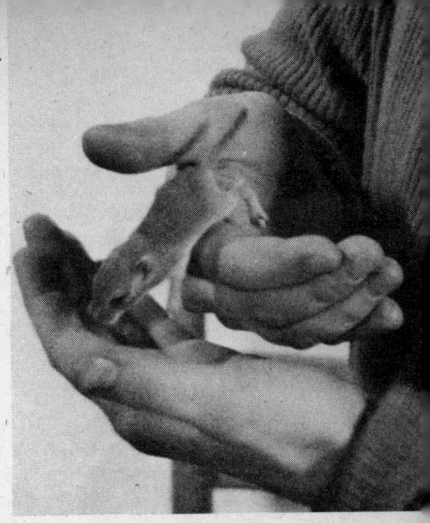

Small, Furry Pets

Some small animals make great pets. You may not be able to ride on their backs, take them for long walks, or expect them to greet you with a purr. But their needs are simple, and they are inexpensive and easy to care for, which makes them good first pets. Of course, as with all animals large or small, the more time you spend together, the more they respond to your care.

Three creatures in this group are not native Americans. The gerbil, the hamster, and the guinea pig were originally brought to the United States from distant lands to be used in laboratories for medical and other research. But soon they proved so easy to get along with that they became popular pets.

They belong to the group of animals called rodents. This means they have front cutting teeth, or incisors, which never stop growing, so they never stop gnawing.

Gerbils are tiny animals about four inches fully grown, with a four-inch tail and short brown fur. Their native home is the desert; they live in the sandy stretches of Africa, Israel, Arabia, and parts of the Soviet Union and Mongolia. All the gerbils living in the United States have been bred from gerbils brought over from the Gobi Desert of Mongolia.

Hamsters are a little bigger and a little chubbier than gerbils, with almost no tail. They have soft fine fur in many shades of brown, pale cream, or light fawn color, all with bright black eyes. They were imported from Syria in the Middle East where they live in deep burrows on dry rocky terrain.

Guinea Pigs are not pigs, and they do not come from Guinea. They are cavies, South American rodents, who

Sophie, a five-year-old guinea pig, likes to eat in comfort.

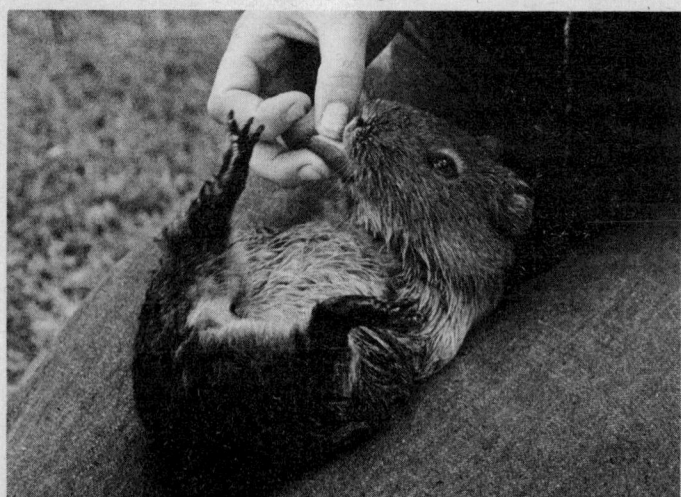

came originally from the dry areas of the Andes Mountains in Peru, where there is not much vegetation. They weigh a pound or more, have short legs, and are about the same size around in front as in the back, so that if you are looking at a long-haired guinea pig, you cannot always tell which is which — unless he is eating! Their hair can be short or long, smooth or rough, and comes in many colors — black, light brown, dark brown, cream, white, either solid or mixed.

Other small mammals which make good pets are mice and rats, both of which are rodents, and rabbits, which are similar to rodents but have different teeth so are called lagomorphs.

Mice, rats, and rabbits of many varieties flourish all over the United States and in virtually every country in the world. However, the pet varieties have been bred for years for special strains.

Pet Mice are about the same size as gerbils. The pure white kind with pink eyes is the most common, but many are bred with coats of all different colors. Mice can be black, blue, chocolate, silver, red, fawn, and champagne in solid colors as well as tan underneath.

Pet Rats are somewhat larger than pet mice. Like mice, they have been bred in many colors, including the albino white rat which has pink eyes. People sometimes frown when you talk of rats as pets, but if you start with baby ones they can be friendly and full of play.

Pet Rabbits. There are now over fifty varieties, more than any other domesticated animal except for dogs. The most popular are the white rabbit and the Dutch rabbit, which can be black, brown, blue or gray, with white markings on nose and feet and across the back like a saddle. There are Angora rabbits with long silky hair, Checkered Giants, which are white with dark splotches, others with short coats like velvet or satin or silver fox, and the lop-eared rabbits with droopy ears twelve inches long.

Grown rabbits can weigh from three to six pounds. They are larger than other small-mammal pets and very nervous. They are easily scared and might scratch or kick. Easy does it: approach them quietly, talk to

Kevin's two-year-old rabbit is one of a fancy breed called Checkered Giant.

them softly, stroke them. NEVER PICK THEM UP BY THEIR EARS. Lift them by the loose skin at the back of the neck with one hand, and put the other hand under the hindquarters to support them.

Whenever you are handling these small animals, try to put yourself in their place and realize how absolutely gigantic you must appear to them. Imagine if somebody came over to you, thrust a huge hand in front of your face, and expected you to climb into the palm — without being scared to death!

If you have read *Gulliver's Travels* by Jonathan Swift, perhaps you will remember that his first voyage of discovery was made to the land of Lilliput, where the people were so tiny he could pick them up by the handful. Well, the second imaginary voyage he made was to the land of Brobdingnab, where the people were so enormous he was terrified even though they meant him no harm. When they picked him up and held him in front of their eyes to look more closely at him, he was scared stiff he might fall to the ground which was so far away to him. At the same time he hurt badly from the pressure of their giant thumbs and fingers. When they spoke, their voice sounded like a rushing torrent, and when they laughed he was nearly deafened.

Read the book and it will give you a good idea how little mice and gerbils and hamsters feel if you are not very very gentle with them.

They are adaptable little creatures, but there are certain things essential to know about their needs.

HOUSING

There are all types of plastic or metal cages in pet stores which are suitable for gerbils, hamsters, mice, and rats. Or you can try building your pets' homes yourself, if you like construction work. In that case, you must make them large enough for exercising, for sleeping quarters, and for providing playthings like ladders and wheels. You must be able to change the food and water easily and to keep the cage clean.

Rabbits and guinea pigs, who need more space, can have wooden hutches for indoors or outdoors. These can be bought ready-made or built at home if you are handy with hammer, wood, and nails. If the hutch has a wire floor — which is a good idea in order to let the droppings fall through — you should put a piece of wood

Here is a very good setup for gerbils. These plastic cages can be added to; they have enough space for an exercise wheel, inverted water bottles, upper floors for food, and plenty of shavings on the floor.

over one section for the animals to rest on, or provide a wooden shelf. It is not good for them to walk on the wire all the time. Since rabbits and guinea pigs are not climbers, they do not need a high house, but they do need enough space for a run.

Whether your pets live inside or out, their houses must be kept free from dampness and drafts. They need fresh air and some sunshine, warmth but not stifling conditions — the same comfortable arrangements you like for yourself.

And since these are gnawing animals, a wooden cage should be lined with hardware cloth inside to prevent the inhabitant from eating his way out — particularly with rats and hamsters.

Whatever kind of home you provide for your pets, don't crowd them. They need room to run around. Mice, rats, and gerbils like toys, small simple things like the core of a roll of toilet paper, an empty reel of thread, or a nut. You can buy more elaborate toys like ladders and wheels and swings from a pet store, but do not clutter up the cage. Leave room for food, water, and bedding.

Shredded newspaper, paper towels, or cat litter make good coverings for the floor. And with rabbits and guinea pigs you should, if possible, keep a supply of hay in one corner. Whatever you use, it must be changed often enough to be free from unpleasant smells, and the cage should be washed out thoroughly, often enough to keep it sweet and clean.

FEEDING

To keep your pets in good health you must feed them right. Prepared food mixtures and pellets from the pet stores make a good basic diet. There are seed mixtures for gerbils, mouse pellets, rabbit pellets which are good for guinea pigs, too, and hamster pellets which can also be fed to rats. There should always be a supply of dry food on hand, preferably in a food holder or feeder that can be attached to the side of the cage.

In addition, they should have something fresh and green from time to time. A lettuce leaf, a piece of carrot, green carrot tops, a celery stick, a parsley stalk, or a bit of apple are all good for them. Grass cuttings, clover, and dandelion leaves are good for guinea pigs and rabbits.

Always provide fresh water daily, either in a gravity feed bottle attached to the cage for the smaller pets or a heavy container for rabbits and guinea pigs. The important thing is to prevent them from spilling the water and making their quarters damp, which is bad for them.

Since they are gnawing animals, a dog biscuit, crushed or kibbled, helps keep the incisor teeth from growing too long. This should stop them from gnawing the wooden parts of their cages, and spare the legs of

A mouse having a drink from a gravity-flow water bottle. The bottle should have fresh water daily.

your chairs and tables when you let them out for a run.

Hamsters are hoarders, so if you wonder where all the food you gave them has gone, look in the corner where they pile their bedding. The other place they tuck the food away is in their cheek pouches, but those you had better leave alone.

Since these pets like to feed in the peace and quiet of the night, fill their dry food containers each evening. Then during the day you can offer them bits of vegetable, fruit, or greens, whenever you have time to spend with them. This helps tame them. They will get used to eating from your hand and eventually will make it easier for you to pick them up. But do not overfeed them, and do not leave the fresh food lying in the cage long enough to go stale.

HEALTH AND HANDLING

If you provide a properly ventilated house away from drafts and dampness, if you keep it clean and the food and water fresh, your pets should stay healthy. But if you think they have caught a cold, which they sometimes do, or show other signs of distress, it is best to ask the vet about them. He will tell you if it is necessary to take an animal to him or whether you can give your pet simple treatment yourself.

The small pets do not need much grooming. They are very good at keeping themselves clean, but a long-haired guinea pig does like a good soft brushing, and so does a rabbit.

It is much kinder to these little creatures, and more fun for you, if you can learn to handle them and let them out of their cages from time to time. Start when they are young, but don't thrust your hand into the cage and expect the animal to snuggle down in your palm. He is likely to give you a sharp nip, simply because he is frightened. Just let him grow used to seeing you about. Animals that are isolated will never get friendly. They will always remain nervous with you, so talk to them, offer a little carrot or lettuce through the wire and wait to see if they are bold enough to take it from you.

When you first open the cage door to let them out, go slowly, quietly, carefully, and wear an old glove, at least to begin with.

Mice, rats, gerbils, and hamsters, given time and kindness, should all venture onto your open hand. Put the other hand over their bodies. Don't squeeze them; stroke them gently. When they get to know you better, don't be alarmed if they run all over you. Gerbils are jumpers, so be prepared. Take care they do not fall, play with them on a rug or blanket on the floor, after making sure doors and windows are shut. Spend some time with your pets each day, let them out, but do not keep them in your hands too long. The moisture and heat is not good for them.

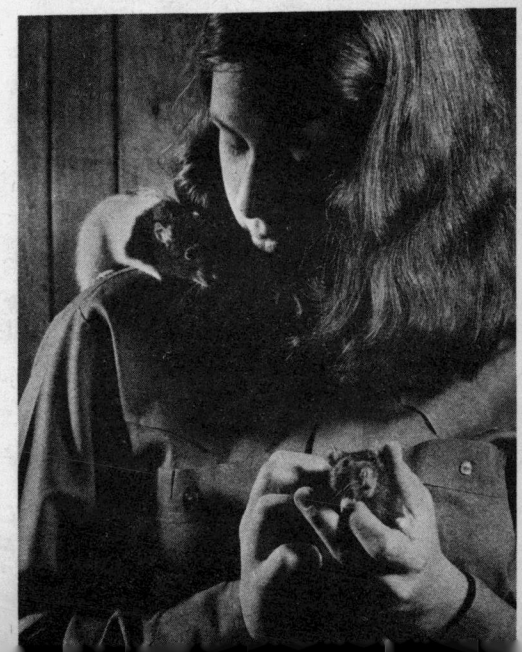

Jeri has two black-and-white rats she calls Winky and Dinky. They were born in her school biology lab. Now they live at home with her, along with three dogs and a turtle.

Rabbits and guinea pigs, once they get to know you, can be picked up gently in both hands, held in your lap and stroked. It is best to do this in an enclosed area. Have an old towel ready to drop on them if they try to amble off.

FAMILY LIFE

When you start with these small pets, it is wise to decide just how many you can look after properly. A single one is easily well housed and cared for, but may get lonely. You can get two of the same sex to keep each other company, but two males together will sometimes fight, especially hamsters. If their house is big enough they will probably get along, but you will have to put them in separate cages if they do not.

If you keep male and female you should be prepared for the families they may have. They can produce a lot of little ones in a short time. They can have several litters a year, from three or four to eight or nine each time.

One reason these animals breed so rapidly is that they have short lives. If there were not a lot of new ones born each year, they would soon die out. Hamsters usually live not more than two years, gerbils, mice and rats may live for four or five, rabbits about the same, and some guinea pigs have been known to reach the age of eight.

If you are going to raise young ones, your first concern should be for the mother. She needs extra food before the babies are born and while she is nursing them. A good addition to her diet is a slice of whole wheat bread crumbled into a small bowl of milk once a day.

She will also want nesting material. Provide extra bedding — straw, hay, shredded paper, wood shavings, or dried grass. When the time for having the young draws near, the mother will busy herself making a nest. If she is a guinea pig or a rabbit she will want a nest box, too. The mother rabbit will add some of her own fur to line the box along with whatever you provide. And a gerbil mother-to-be loves scraps of cloth so she can make shreds to arrange around the nest to her liking.

A gerbil mother with some of her family. When making a nest, a gerbil mother likes a piece of soft cloth to tear up and add to the bedding.

With hamsters and rats, you should take the male away from the female before the babies are born and while she is nursing them. The male is likely to harass the mother, then either she or the father will eat the young. Once the babies are weaned, that is, ready to eat the same food as their parents, you have new problems. More cages are needed, boys must be separated from girls and, most important, good homes must be found for the new-comers you do not want to keep yourself.

It is not easy to determine at exactly what age this separating and sorting and giving away should be done. It can vary considerably. Find out in advance, from the pet store where you bought the parents, or from the people who reared them, just what they did to breed the families successfully. There are quite a few problems in raising animal families in confined spaces, and even zoos haven't got all the answers.

A Pet Bird

It is hard to imagine what the world would be like without birds — no ducks on the ponds, no gulls in the harbors, no shore birds at the water's edge, none of the bright flashes of innumerable birds in fields and woods and along country roads. No flocks of sparrows and pigeons busy in the city squares and on the rooftops, and no strange creatures like the pelicans and penguins at the zoo!

And how quiet it would be with no birds singing through the day, no owls hooting in the night!

Hard to imagine, yet bird life is in danger.

With the spread of towns, factories, and thousands of miles of paved roads, plus vast acreage of drained wetlands and the invasion of wilderness areas, there is increasing encroachment on the habitats of birds every year. And those who somehow manage still have to face the dangers of pesticides and detergent waste.

One of the many varieties of bird feeders you can set up in your garden.

Fortunately for the birds, most are persistent and adaptable. They will go on mating and nest-building and rearing their young in the face of many difficulties. Most of them, that is — but not all. Some, like the once numerous Passenger Pigeon, have completely disappeared, and others are on the danger list.

Fortunately there is a brighter side to the picture. Nowadays, there is a much greater understanding of the need for conservation, which includes survival space for birds and other wildlife.

And there are federal and state laws aimed at protecting the bird population. Many birds are profiting —

and so are we, since a lot of them feed almost entirely on plant and insect pests which harm our food crops.

In most states it is illegal to catch and cage any of our native wild birds. There are some exceptions, and regulations vary, so it is best to check the Conservation Department in your state to acquaint yourself with the bird laws in your area. Cage birds that are kept in cages and aviaries now have been imported from other parts of the world; their descendants have been bred in captivity here.

THE CROW

The crow is still unprotected in most places. He has, whether he deserves it or not, a bad reputation. Although he helps tidy up the countryside by eating carrion, it's true that he also likes the eggs and chicks of other birds as well as the farmer's grain, and these tastes make him unpopular.

Noisy, thieving, and impudent, he can still make an interesting pet. A young one can be tamed and given the freedom of your home, if you do not mind a lot of noise, some mess, and his habit of helping himself to small bright objects lying around. Tamed and talked to, he makes a lively companion. He chuckles and whistles and can be taught a few words, but he should *never* have his tongue split. The idea that this makes him talk more is old-fashioned nonsense; it is cruel, and there is no reason for it ever to be done.

THE FINCHES

Finches are one of the largest families in the bird world, with a great variety of members. Some of the most brightly colored birds in the United States, like the cardinals, the grosbeaks, and the buntings, belong to the finch family, with beaks adapted for seed-cracking. And so (in spite of their duller feathers) do the various sparrows.

A host of tiny domesticated finches in all colors of the rainbow come from Australia, Africa, and Asia. These are the birds you see in pet stores. They are not very tuneful, they just twitter, but they are bright little splashes of color which are a joy to watch and to care for.

The vocalists of the finch family are the canaries. Originally they came from the Canary Islands off the west coast of Africa. Since then they have traveled far and been reared in many countries. The finest singer is the roller canary. It was first bred in the Harz Mountains of Germany, where the young were trained to trill by listening to their elders. You can encourage your young canary to sing by playing a song recording which is available at pet stores.

Most of these birds are hardy, but they still need to be well cared for.

Housing. Each kind of bird needs the right cage, one large enough to fly in and to stretch its wings. The

This elegant cage houses Stephen's cockateel. He is trying to get the bird to talk by running the tape recorder (on top of cage at left). It says "Hello! Tito!" over and over again.

perches and bars must be right, too. The bird's claws must be able to grip the perches comfortably, and the bars must be close enough together to prevent the bird from flying through. The tiny finches would disappear from a cage intended for a larger bird.

A leafless branch from a tree can be placed inside the cage, but should not be so large that it crowds the bird out, and there must be room for the containers of food and water.

All birds need some sunshine and some shade. But do not leave them where they will bake or shiver, protect them from drafts, and put a cover over them at nighttime. If you want your bird to be healthy and happy, be sure the cage is kept fresh and clean.

Diet. These birds need a daily supply of the right seed mixture and grit, both of which you can get from pet stores or supermarkets. They should also have some greenery several times a week. It must be fresh and should be removed if it goes stale before they have eaten it. Anything like celery, carrot tops, lettuce, chickweed, or dandelion leaves is good for them, or you can buy special pots of sprouting seeds. A piece of cuttlebone should be kept where they can get at it. This is the inner shell of the cuttlefish and obtainable at pet stores. The birds need it to trim their beaks.

Water must be fresh and in a container they will not spill or make dirty. A shallow flowerpot saucer with an inch or two of water will let them take a weekly bath. If they don't like the bath, occasionally try a gentle spray.

THE PARROT FAMILY

This is another family of brilliantly colored lively birds that come from different parts of the world and make fine pets. Some may not be imported into the United States because they are disease carriers, but several varieties have been here for a long time, are bred in the United States, and flourish.

Perhaps the favorite is the shell parakeet, often known by its Australian name, budgerigar, or budgie for short. Originally bright green little birds with long tails, they now come in a range of colors: green, blue, yellow, even violet. Also originating in Australia is the cockateel, a somewhat larger bird, but one of the gentlest, chattiest, and easiest to tame. They are more expensive to buy and need a larger cage.

Then there are the lovebirds, which are a little smaller than a budgie and have a shorter tail. Originally from Africa, they too come in a beautiful variety of soft colors and have very pleasing ways.

With any of these birds you must decide whether you want to keep a single one, or whether you want a pair or more so that you can try breeding them. If you are interested in taming your bird and getting him to talk, you should keep only one.

Whichever you decide, whether you get one bird or an aviary full, seeing that they get proper care and attention is a daily job. Be sure to get a roomy cage, equip it properly, and keep it clean. Aside from the containers for food, grit, and water, the birds enjoy a little furniture in their homes — a ladder to climb, a bell to ring, or a mirror to preen in front of.

Diet. Give them a parakeet seed mixture daily and check the container to remove the empty hulls they leave. In addition, leave a fresh piece of celery, apple, or carrot several times a week, and keep a piece of cuttlebone handy for their beaks. Keep their water fresh, even if they do not drink much of it, and offer them a bath occasionally in a flowerpot saucer containing a couple of inches of water. If they ignore the bath, try spraying them gently with an atomizer.

Training. If you are interested in taming your bird and teaching him to say a few words, start with a young one and preferably a male. Wait until he has settled into his new home, but talk to him quietly whenever you are near so he gets used to you.

To teach him to perch on your finger, open the cage and slowly put your hand in. Press your hand with forefinger outstretched gently against the bird's breast; gradually he will get the idea and step onto your finger. Keep it up for a few days and then, with the bird settled on your finger, draw your hand slowly out of the cage. Make sure all doors and windows are shut before you start. He will enjoy the freedom of flying around the room and in time may return to the cage of his own accord. Or he may perch on your outstretched finger and you can put him back that way. If you have any trouble putting him back, don't chase him all over the room. Leave the cage door open and wait for him to grow tired. When he finally settles down, drop a towel over him and pick him up gently in it.

To teach him to whistle, say his name, your name, or other words. Keep repeating the sound or the word to him as he sits on your finger or each time you pass by his cage. When you first get your bird you cannot tell whether he is going to be a good talker. Birds vary very much in this ability. You can only try to teach him, and if he does not get very far, he can still be fun and learn other tricks.

DOVES

Doves are excellent birds to keep as pets. They seem content to sit on their perches and gently coo, either singly or in pairs, and they are equally peaceful in an aviary with other birds around them. However, they do not get on particularly with other doves; two breeding pairs, if left together, will very likely quarrel. It is

This dove was released by someone out of the picture to fly to its owner's hand. A slow flash allowed the wings to blur.

best to keep breeding pairs in separate cages, and no doubt they will busy themselves raising families.

There are three varieties in most pet stores. There is the white dove, sometimes called the sacred dove; the ringneck, with light fawn feathers and a black collar band; and the diamond dove, smaller than the other two, and slate-blue in color.

They are all attractive, friendly, and easy to care for. They will eat most of the seed mixtures prepared for the other birds, like finches or parakeets, and they need the same grit, too.

They can be taught to perch on your finger, but are usually content to return to the security of their cage.

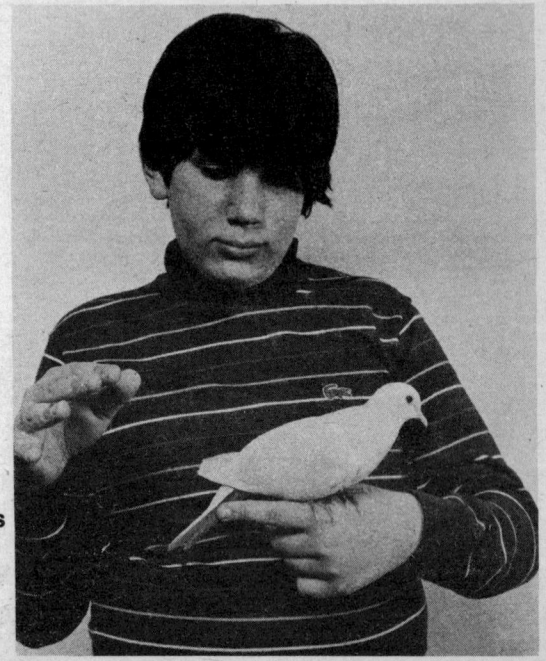

One of the white doves perching on Stephen's finger.

THE MYNAH BIRD

A bird that you can be pretty sure will talk is a mynah. They come from India, they are not very pretty (their black plumage often looks untidy) but they love to imitate sounds and voices and often learn several words and even sentences. They are friendly, amusing, and not difficult to care for.

Diet and Care. Mynah birds will eat almost anything whether it is good or bad for them. The best diet for them is mynah food from the pet store, varied with chopped hard-boiled egg, a little raw ground meat, and fruit. They are fond of all fruit, but they are not seedeaters.

The cage can get messy, so use sheets of newspaper beneath and inside and change the paper often.

Mynahs like to take a bath in a shallow dish of water, and they like to spread their wings in the sunshine.

And like all other cage birds, they need fresh water to drink at all times.

Snakes as Pets

Snakes as pets? Although they are not furry and cuddly, many people find them responsive—in their own way. If you have a snake as a pet, you know you are not able to slip a collar over its head and take it for a walk; it will not come running to the door to greet you when you get home, and you cannot coax it to be friendly by offering tidbits, for it will only be interested in eating about once every ten days—if then.

Snakes are members of the reptile class. Their habits and needs are very different from those of mammals and birds. As a result, snakes seem very remote from us and are often much misunderstood.

Here are some useful facts about snakes:

Body temperature and surface. Snakes are cold-blooded creatures. This means that their bodies are about the same temperature as their surroundings. In the sun they feel warm and dry to the touch. In cold weather snakes are cold and do not move easily.

Ears. Snakes have no ears, but probably hear some sound through the inner bony structure. Snakes may appear to sway to the rhythm of a snake-charmer's flute, but actually their eyes are following the movements of the charmer.

Tongue. A snake's forked tongue is not for stinging. The snake is not about to bite when its tongue flickers in and out. A snake smells with its tongue. The organ is sensitive to surrounding odors, and the snake's tongue tells it whether there is food or danger in the area.

Locomotion. Snakes have no legs to walk or climb with. They use their ribs, which are constructed so that with the aid of the scales on their undersides, the snake can push its way along. The scales must keep in contact with the ground or tree for this method to work, so snakes do not progress in loops like a caterpillar. They slither along.

Snakeskins. Over their scales and even their eyes, snakes wear a transparent skin which they shed several times a year. The whole skin comes off in one piece.

When the time comes for shedding, the snake will start the process by rubbing its nose against rock or bark, which helps to loosen the old skin around the mouth. Then it will squirm about, rub against twigs or stones, and gradually the whole skin comes off—inside out. And underneath the snake has a beautiful new coat.

CHOOSING YOUR SNAKE

As pets, snakes are not likely to be satisfactory if you are looking for affection and friendliness. Some snakes tolerate being handled, and some show awareness of the person who feeds them. However, one well-known snake expert tells the story of a man who thought his rattler knew him but found it depended on which jacket he wore. Apparently the snake recognized one particular coat but reacted as though the man were a stranger when he wore a different one!

If you are really interested in observing and learning about snakes, it is a good idea to get one. Some people have snakes as pets just because they like to be different, and they are not as concerned with the snake as they are with themselves. This is not a particularly good reason for keeping snakes.

Snakes do have one advantage over warm-blooded pets. They do not demand such constant care. With proper housing kept clean and at the right temperature, with proper food and water supplies, they can be left alone much of the time.

Boa constrictors. These snakes, from the warmer parts of South America, are popular for home care and are obtainable in many pet stores.

Housing. Your boa does not need a great deal of room to roam—naturally, as it grows it may need larger

Suzanne brings her brother's pet snake to school. This is a boa constrictor, native of the warmer parts of South America. B.C., as it is called, is about three years old and three feet long. Boas can grow much bigger.

quarters—but it does need warmth, freedom from drafts, some sun occasionally, and an arrangement within the cage where it can get out of sight.

An aquarium fitted with a fine screen top, which can be securely fastened, will do if the aquarium is properly equipped. It should contain a thermometer, and the temperature should stay between 75° and 80°F. A good way to provide constant warmth is to install a shaded incandescent light bulb. A twenty-five watt bulb should be enough for two cubic feet, higher wattage for a larger area. The best idea is to get the cage before you get the snake and experiment until you are sure the temperature will remain constant at 75° or a little over. Or you can install a terrarium (not aquarium) thermostat. You can find this at the stores that keep aquarium supplies for tropical fish.

A good cage can be made of wood and glass. It should have a solid wooden floor and back, wood sides with small panels of screen wire for ventilation, and a sliding glass front. It can also have a lift-up top with a secure fastening.

At home, Suzanne does her homework while the boa moves around. In the background you can see the aquarium where it lives with a larger boa, Lucille, who is five feet long.

The bottom of the cage can have cat litter, gravel, or paper, but must be kept clean and dry. Fortunately this is not difficult. Since snakes do not eat often, they don't excrete often either.

Although the boa does not need a lot of room to move about, the cage must be big enough to contain a hiding place. An inverted cardboard box with a cutout entrance will work, as long as the box is big enough for the boa to coil up inside.

Also there should be room for a fixed branch or piece of driftwood for climbing, and a shallow pan of water, fresh each day. The pan should be roomy enough for the boa to soak in when it is about to shed its skin. The shedding is an interesting process, but never attempt to help the snake. It is a sign of a healthy snake if the skin comes off in one piece.

Feeding. Boas' appetites vary, but they usually like to eat once every seven to ten days. They may indicate that they are getting interested in food by showing more activity than usual.

A newcomer may be ready to eat but still refuse to do so if it is being watched. Later it may grow more relaxed about eating, but it should never be handled while eating.

Boas as a rule prefer live food. A mouse makes an adequate meal for a young boa, a rat when the boa grows larger. The prey is killed almost instantaneously by the constriction of the boa's coils. It is then swallowed whole and the boa retires to digest the meal.

Some herpetologists, that is, snake scientists, say experience shows it is possible to feed boas dead food. But the boa still needs the whole animal, so it can be given dead mice, rats, or other small rodents, and possibly it will accept small raw chicken parts.

Handling. Let your boa grow used to its new surroundings before you attempt much handling. To begin with, always hold it just behind the head. As you lift it gently from the cage, support the body with your other hand. If it feels that it is going to fall it will get scared and thrash around, but once it gains confidence you can let it wander. However, before you let it roam, make sure there are no handy cracks or crevices or openings where it can escape.

Our Native Snakes. You need not go to a pet shop to get a snake, since there are plenty of native American varieties for you to discover. If you go snake hunting, start out with an old pillowcase to bring your friends home in and a stick for turning over stones before you know what is under them, and wear boots.

The most common are the garter and ribbon snakes which you may find in old tree stumps, under rocks or stones, in the woods, or in open country. They are harmless and so are other common varieties, like De Kay's snake, the milk snake, the ringnecked snake, and the western rubber boa.

If you have someone with you who can assure you that your find is harmless, pick him up and put him in your bag. You need to know what kind he is in order to take care of him properly, so identify him as soon as you can. There are illustrated books on snakes in school and public libraries, if you haven't one of your own at home.

If he is a garter, ribbon, smooth green, ringnecked, or De Kay's snake, or a western rubber boa, he is not likely to grow longer than two feet. If he is a milk snake he may reach three feet.

Except for the milk snake, which is a constrictor and needs to be fed live mice or rats, you can catch crickets and other insects to offer your snake. And most of them will settle for chopped raw liver or raw fish, particularly the guts of the fish which we do not usually eat ourselves.

The same housing that is suitable for a pet store boa will be fine for other snakes, but if yours is a native American, he will not need a heated cage. Try to reproduce the sort of terrain you found him in, and be sure to provide the snake with a cubbyhole for hiding.

Toads, Frogs, Turtles, or Lizards as Pets

In your wanderings you may come across other members of the reptile family, like lizards or turtles. Or you may find some of their near relatives, the frogs and toads, who are amphibians, which means they spend their lives both on land and in water.

Lizards. Various kinds of fence lizard are common, and you may often see them basking in the sun. But you must be quick to catch a lizard. If you take one home and want him to flourish, he needs a dry but airy house where he can get a lot of sunlight. He will eat flies and most other insects, but if you are not able to catch enough of them, you can get mealworms from the pet store.

Salamanders. You may find salamanders—small, bright-orange or spotted, lizardlike creatures—in moist places or after a rain. These are not true lizards, but amphibians. They are scaleless, with soft moist skin, and breathe by gills in the larval stage. They should not be treated like lizards, but more like frogs.

Turtles. Turtles are fairly easy to care for, as long as they have enough water for a swim and a ledge to sit and dry themselves in the sun. Feed turtles chopped raw meat or fish, and they should have some fresh lettuce leaves or other green plant material.

Should you get a tiny hand-decorated turtle (which you will certainly not find in the countryside, but for sale swimming in a tank) he will make you a fine pet. The first thing to do is to remove his decoration! Wipe his shell carefully with a small pad of cotton soaked in lacquer thinner or acetone. Be sure not to get *any* liquid on the turtle or on you.

The turtle in the photograph started out with a painted shell some years ago. He now lives happily in his natural colors outdoors in warm weather, indoors in

Originally, this was a tiny turtle with a painted shell which somebody threw away five years ago. Turtles shed their carapace, or shell, in sections. Jeri points to one that is about to come off.

Left, Chip gently holds a young bullfrog — or that's what he thinks it is. He will look it up at home. *Right,* Chip with a box turtle he has also found in the marshland. He holds it so it cannot bite.

the winter. He has a small dry house of his own and takes a swim in an aquarium full of tropical fish. He feeds on chopped meat and greenstuff, and the fish are smart enough and quick enough to keep out of his way. Otherwise, if hungry, he might eat them.

Frogs and Toads. While snakes, apart from an occasional hiss, are silent creatures, frogs and toads are very vocal.

The smallest ones, the spring peepers, which are scarcely one inch long, make some of the loudest noises, a shrill lively chorus on a spring or summer evening.

Then there are the bass singers, the bullfrogs, the

largest growing seven to eight inches in length. The male, who is the vocal one, keeps repeating "jug-o-rum, jug-o-rum," his mating call, while he lurks in the pondside vegetation.

Like the frogs, a number of toads are singers, too, and they are all useful creatures because they are insect eaters.

If you want to watch them more closely and can take one home, a small outdoor pool is the best place to keep it — if it will stay there. If you take frogs or toads indoors you must provide them with a proper container like a terrarium or an aquarium. Feed them earthworms, insects, and mealworms. A bullfrog in captivity is best kept alone, as he will eat any other frog or toad that is small enough for him to swallow.

Having taken wild creatures from their own homes, it is only fair that you feed and house them properly. If

A bullfrog on a partly submerged tree limb. Quiet at this moment, he has a loud bass voice when he starts his call.

they do not seem able to adapt to the setup you offer, the kindest thing is to return them to their natural surroundings.

Whichever living creatures you bring home, whether they are mammals, birds, reptiles or amphibians, whether they were tamed by man or are still living free, the decision has been yours, not theirs. You and they may run into problems about living together, but if you put yourself in their place you will work things out between you. They will have a good life and you will have all sorts of rewards and surprises that you never dreamed of.